TRASH ANIMALS

Live Free, Eat Trash!

Written by
Alexander Schneider

RP Minis®
Hachette Book Group
1290 Avenue of the Americas, New York, NY 10104
www.runningpress.com
@Running_Press

First Edition: October 2023

Published by RP Minis, an imprint of Perseus Books, LLC, a subsidiary of
Hachette Book Group, Inc. The RP Minis name and logo is a registered
trademark of the Hachette Book Group.

Running Press books may be purchased in bulk for business, educationa
or promotional use. For more information, please contact your local
bookseller or the Hachette Book Group Special Markets Department at
Special.Markets@hbgusa.com.

The publisher is not responsible for websites (or their content) that are n
owned by the publisher.

ISBN: 978-0-7624-8431-7

CONTENTS

Hey garbage friends! In this mini kit, you'll find 25 magnets of your favorite trash animals and the perfect double-sided backdrop to create fun scenes. These lovable creatures have so much to teach us about the world. Check out their profiles and some amazingly kooky facts.

These affectionately labeled Trash Pandas get their English name from the Powhatan word *Aroughcun*, which means "one that scratches with its hands." Those hands make up for poor eyesight and potential color blindness with five times more sensory cells in their paws than most other mammals. They can practically see an object through touch!

Raccoons' natural mask provides what evolutionary advantage?

- **A.** Likeness to a purple fast-food criminal
- **B.** An individualized identity marker
- **C.** Glare reduction
- **D.** Ward off predators

ANSWER: C. Their black rings reduce glare, helping their nighttime criminal behavior.

LITTLE SMARTIES

Humans continue to improve raccoons' adaptability and problem-solving skills by forcing them to navigate manufactured obstacles. City-faring raccoons have a paw up on their rural neighbors.

TRUE OR FALSE: Raccoons are naturally slow-moving mammals.

ANSWER: False–raccoons can run at speeds of up to 15 miles per hour!

Akin to human hands, raccoons have five dexterous toes on their front paws that can successfully navigate twisting handles, opening trash cans, and maybe sliding into those DMs. Idle hands, etc.

NIGHT-NIGHT TINY BANDIT

Raccoons don't hibernate but remain in their dens for weeks at a time during winter. This state of torpor lowers their body temperature and metabolism, reducing energy usage and food intake. Torpor would make a great vacation idea.

What two animals can pass the Aesop's Fable test? (A test commonly used to test animal intelligence.)

A. Crow

B. Fox

C. Rat

D. Raccoon

ANSWERS: A & D. The Aesop's Fable test is based on the story of how a thirsty crow dropped stones into a pitcher to raise the water level to a point where it could drink. A 2017 study showed that two out of eight raccoons tested were able to drop stones into a tube with water to snag a floating marshmallow. A third raccoon simply tipped the dang test tube over. No trash can is safe.

Raccoons have a diverse set of calls used for communication and during competitions over food. How many calls have humans noted?

A. 25

B. 50

C. 75

D. 100

ANSWER: B. Raccoons have more than 50 calls, including hissing, high-pitched trills, purrs, guttural growls, and playful chatter.

Male raccoons attempt to mate with
multiple females each season, while female
raccoons generally mate with one partner.

From caring for sick and injured community members to experiencing feelings of loneliness, rats rival humans in both neuroses and humanity. But few see the wonder in them like the Karni Mata Temple in India, home to over 25,000 worshiped black rats! These startling rodent communities maintain a sophisticated social structure complete with leaders, secondary leaders, outcasts, and even rebels! *Have you heard about the*

rat that got a job in politics? She is a
bureauc-rat now.

- Rats are ticklish.
- Rats make sounds similar to laughter when they are happy.
- Rats learn what food they like from smelling the breath of others.
- Rats are clean animals, even cleaner than cats!

BULLYING IS NOT ALRIGHT

Rats will succumb to peer pressure, disregarding personal preference to copy their peers' behavior. Just like humans, the urge to conform can be so strong they will even eat unpalatable food in the presence of other rats. These rat-diculous choices can negatively affect rats in the form of regret.

Although curious, rats are very shy and are what is known as neophobic, meaning they are afraid of trying new things.

THE MAJESTY OF DANCE

These masters of communicators utilize body language, touch, sound, and even smell! They have been used to detect landmines and diagnose diseases such as tuberculosis. Rat-ical!

The human equivalent of a rat jump would be what?

  A. Jumping onto a chair

  B. Jumping onto a one-story building

  C. Jumping onto a three-story building

  D. Jumping into space

ANSWER: B. Rats can jump two feet in the air from a standing position and an additional foot with a running start.

Scientists have identified that rats dream!

Rats' jaws can exert as much as 7,000 pounds per square inch; capable of chewing through glass, cinderblock, wire, aluminum, and lead.

TRUE OR FALSE: Kangaroo rats can survive ten years without water.

ANSWER: True! They can survive their entire life without drinking water!

PIGEON

PROFILE

One of the coo-lest trash animals gets a bad rap for being dirty and disease-ridden, but pigeons are clean animals and groom themselves often. In 16th-century England, their "dirtiest acts" were the best available fertilizer. The high value of pigeon guano required armed guards to protect the royal dovecotes (pigeon houses).

Pigeons can hear frequencies outside the human spectrum, sensing volcanic eruptions and incoming storms

before meteorologists can detect them.
These must be the omen pigeons!

WAR HEROES

Thirty-two pigeons have won the Dickin Medal, an award that honors animal bravery and courage while in military service. The medal was awarded 54 times between 1943 and 1949 to 32 pigeons, 18 dogs, 3 horses, and a ship's cat.

Columbiformes is an order of birds that includes:

A. Mourning Dove
B. Rock Pigeon
C. Dodo
D. Mindanao Bleeding-heart

ANSWER: All of the above—308 living species of pigeons and doves in the Columbiformes order.

Pigeons understand the concepts of both time and space. Humans process those concepts with a region of the brain called the parietal cortex;

pigeon brains lack that cortex, so they have an alternative way of judging that humans have not yet identified.

DON'T MILK IT
TILL YOU TRY IT

Both female and male pigeons share the responsibility of raising their young. They take turns incubating eggs and feeding the chicks "crop milk." Both sexes produce this whitish secretion of nutrients, fats, antioxidants, and healthy proteins in the lining of their crop. Parents typically raise two chicks at a time.

Most birds cannot recognize their own image. Pigeons, however, can identify themselves among photos of different pigeons and even recognize each letter of the alphabet. Their recognition skills don't end there, distinguishing humans within a single photograph. They are one of a small number of species to pass this "mirror test."

SEAGULL

PROFILE

Seagulls are attentive, caring, and monogamous parents. Each mate takes turns incubating eggs, feeding their young, and protecting their chicks. This is no small feat considering their average lifespan is 10–15 years in the wild, with the occasional seagull living up to 30 years.

Their family values extend to sharing the same nesting site for generations! Sadly, this makes them more vulnerable to human disruption and displacement.

You might see these birds as a beach nuisance. But different feeding strategies, such as dropping mollusks onto rocks to break them open and seeking out plowed fields for unearthed grubs and insects, demonstrate their intelligence. Their highly developed communication repertoire includes a variety of vocalizations and body movements. These are just a few vital skills young gulls learn in a nursery flock, led by a select group of adult males, who watch over the flocks until they are old enough to breed.

While seagulls' primary diet consists of seafood, insects, and sea vegetation, they will scavenge human food whenever possible—even the occasional unsuspecting tourist with a bag of french fries.

Seagulls' side-set eyes give them a panoramic view of their surroundings, Perfect for spotting predators from all angles. But how far can they see in any direction?

A. 100 feet

B. 300 yards

C. As the crow flies

D. 2 miles

ANSWER: D. Seagulls have great vision and can see clearly for 2 miles.

While seagulls recognize other seagulls by their unique call, they can identify humans by their faces! Over several days seagulls remember, especially when food is involved, specific people and places. If only they could help us locate our cars in a beach parking lot.

TRUE OR FALSE: Seagulls cannot drink saltwater.

ANSWER: False—seagulls can drink saltwater using salt glands and ducts connected to their bills. This built-in water distillation filter rids their bodies of excess salts.

Seagulls stamp their feet on the ground to:

A. Attract mates with their mastery of spirit feathers

B. Trick earthworms

C. Flatten sand for comfortable roosting

D. Mock their seagull enemies

ANSWER: B. Seagulls pound the ground with their feet imitating rain and tricking earthworms into coming to the surface and their inevitable demise.

JINKIES!

Since these birds are more lovers than fighters, they utilize an erratic flight pattern called "jinking" to confuse predators. Unpredictable and ever-changing trajectories help keep birds with superior speeds like falcons and hawks on the losing side at mealtimes.

SKUNK

These no-no-no-notorious creatures thrive in diverse habitats across North America. Although uncommon pets, skunk owners love these smart and curious animals that exhibit individual personalities just like dogs and cats. While some have a taste for garbage, their palates are more accustomed to insects, snakes, fruit, and vegetables.

How many ounces of fluid can a skunk hold at one time?

A. One-half ounce

B. Two ounces

C. Five ounces

D. They are smelly demon babies with an endless supply

ANSWER: B. The 10- to 14-day production of this potentially life-saving substance forces them to fend off threats by other means and only spray when necessary.

HANDSTAND DANCE

While it might sound like a cool trend you see on the internet, it's a threat doled out by our essence-filled friends. Standing on their forelimbs with their tail and hind legs in the air, they ominously aim their scent glands. Stomping, hissing, and charging their target accompany this menacing dance. Cute and terrifying.

Among the strong mamas in the animal kingdom are skunks, who drive off their male after mating to raise 2–12 "kits" alone.

SPRAY SPELL SHEET

- **PLAGUE MIST:** Engulf your threat in a sticky, smelly cloud that lasts for days.
- **CONCENTRATED FIRE:** Focus your stream for a high degree of directional aim.
- **DOUBLE BARREL:** Spray from both glands for a devastating blow, but deplete your supply by 33%.
- **LONG SHOT:** Target a threat over 15 feet away with a significant loss of accuracy.

Not a practical defense mechanism for skunks but helpful in a zombie apocalypse, skunk spray is highly flammable. The spray (n-butyl mercaptan) is composed of thiols similar to the sulfur-based compounds found in garlic and onions. This scent can be detected up to a mile and a half away, unless you are part of the 1 in 1,000 people who are unable to smell their malodorous bouquet.

This book has been bound
using handcraft methods
and Smyth-sewn to
ensure durability.

Designed by
Justine Kelley.